STORYtown

CATCH A WAVE

Harcourt
SCHOOL PUBLISHERS

www.harcourtschool.com

CONTENTS

envisioned

gesture

proportion

resisted

scholars

specialized

Vocabulary

Build Robust Vocabulary

Write the Vocabulary Word that completes each sentence in the letters. The first one has been done for you.

Dear Dora,

We visited the State Capitol in Sacramento, California. I was looking forward to seeing the tile floor that was restored in the 1970s. Many **(1)** ___scholars___ have said that the floor is a work of art. I wanted to see for myself. I had **(2)** _____ it as something grand. It was! At first, Dan **(3)** _____ our attempts to get him to tour the Capitol. Now he is glad he went. I'll tell you more details in my next letter.

Your pal,
Flor

Dear Dora,

Here are just a few more notes from our tour of the California State Capitol. In the 1970s, a man named Hans Scharff had to clean each floor tile by hand. He was an artist that **(4)** _____ in tile.

What a chore! He took up each tile from the floor in order to clean them one by one. Then he had to put each of the tiles back down again. The tiles had to be in the same order they had been in before. The **(5)** _____ of the tiles had to be the same, too.

It was a big job, but Scharff finished the tile floor. Then he took off the sheets in a grand **(6)** _____ , as if to show how perfect it was. I have some prints to show you when we get home. You'll be amazed!

Your pal,
Flor

THE TILE FLOOR

by Emily Hutchinson • illustrated by Shadra Strickland

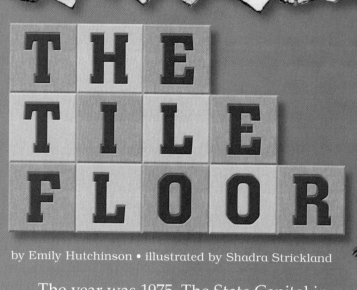

The year was 1975. The State Capitol in California had been in use for more than one hundred years. It was no longer safe. The brick walls could fall down, so the problem couldn't be ignored.

The Capitol needed to be torn down or restored. It was hard to think of what to do. All who envisioned a grand State Capitol wanted to restore it. **1**

Stop and Think

1 What is the problem with the Capitol? How could it be solved?

The problem is _____

It could be solved by _____

_____

All the walls and floors had to be torn out. Then stronger ones could go in. The upper floor had more problems. The marble floor was like art. In fact, some art scholars said it was indeed art. It dated from 1906. They resisted a plan to get rid of it. How could it be saved? ❷

Small marble tiles covered the floor of the Capitol.

Stop and Think

❷ What do you think will happen to the marble floor?

I think the marble floor will _____

_____

_____

It was going to be hard, but the floor could be saved. It was scored and cut into parts. Then the parts were stuck to big boards. When the boards were lifted, the parts came up. Then the tiles were taken off the boards, one at a time. Now someone needed to clean all those tiles. **3**

Stop and Think

3 Why do you think the tiles were taken off one at a time?

I think the tiles _____

_____

_____

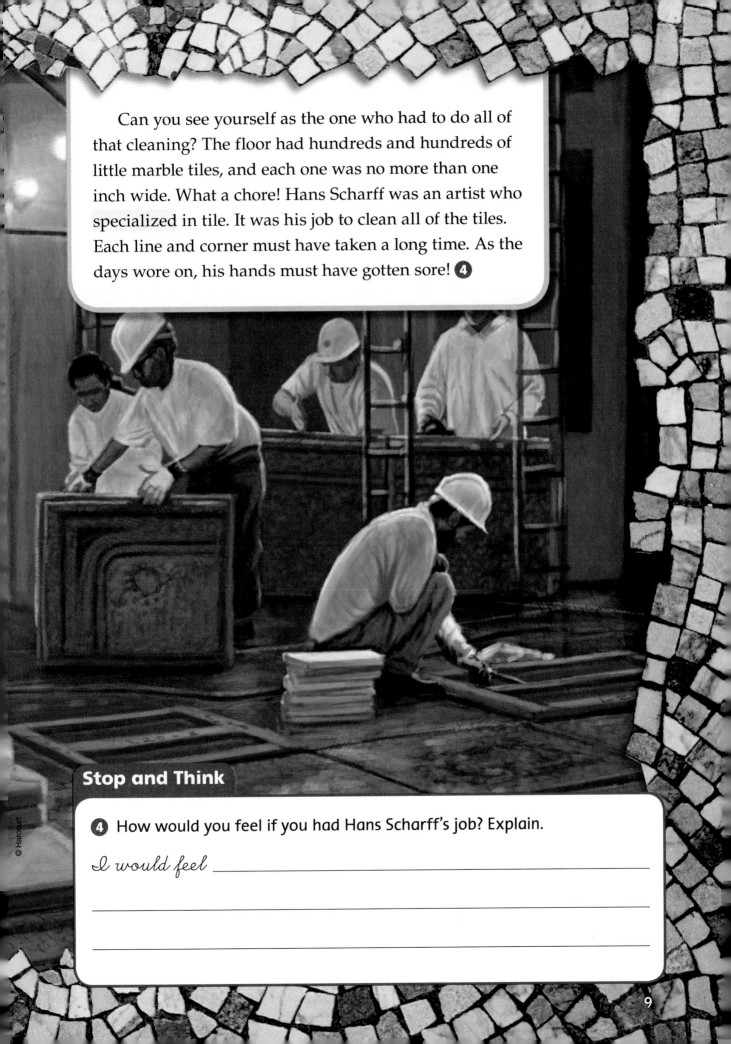

Can you see yourself as the one who had to do all of that cleaning? The floor had hundreds and hundreds of little marble tiles, and each one was no more than one inch wide. What a chore! Hans Scharff was an artist who specialized in tile. It was his job to clean all of the tiles. Each line and corner must have taken a long time. As the days wore on, his hands must have gotten sore! **4**

Stop and Think

4 How would you feel if you had Hans Scharff's job? Explain.

I would feel _____

_____

_____

After all that cleaning, Hans still had more chores to do. He poured paste on big sheets. He set the tiles on the paste in the same order and proportion. Then he let the paste set. These tile-covered sheets were stored in boxes. All of the sheets were sent by train back to the Capitol. It was time to complete the floor. **5**

Workers carefully cleaned and restored the marble tiles.

Stop and Think

5 What did Hans Scharff do after cleaning the tiles?

After cleaning the tiles, Hans Scharff _____

_____

_____

More was in store for those tiles! The next task was to set the tiles on the upper hall floor. When the tiles were set, off came the sheets in a grand gesture. The job was finished! At last, the marble floor was complete. **6**

Stop and Think

6 Do you think it was a good idea to restore the tile floor? Explain.

I think that _____

_____

_____

Now, *you* can explore the State Capitol. Your trip will take you past the marble floor. You can see how well it was restored. You can see how grand this marble floor is. Then you'll understand just how all that hard work paid off! **7**

Stop and Think

7 What did you learn about in this selection?

I learned about _____

_____

_____

Think Critically

1. What is the main idea of this selection? **MAIN IDEA**

The main idea is that _____

_____

_____

2. What were the last steps in restoring the tile floor? Copy the chart, and fill it in. **SEQUENCE**

Event 1
The tiles were sent back to the Capitol.

Event 2

Event 3

3. How is the new Capitol like the old one? How is it different?
COMPARE AND CONTRAST

It's like the old one because _____

_____

It's different because _____

_____

_____

broached

conducted

dignified

inflammable

rowdy

seldom

shatter

Vocabulary

Build Robust Vocabulary

Write the Vocabulary Word that completes each sentence in the postcards. The first one has been done for you.

Dear Julie,

I'm on a neat ship! My dad is teaching history to the university students. Last week, he **(1)** ___conducted___ classes on the deck. Classes at sea are fun. We learn a lot! This morning, I learned how **(2)** _____ objects catch on fire. I'll explain it when I get back.

Your friend at sea,

Tony

Julie Steel

1424 Main Street

Stamford, CT 06901

Dear Patrick,

I made some friends on the ship. Their parents are professors like my dad. There are a lot of university students on the ship, too. The older students often get wild and **(3)** _____ ! My friends and I do our best to act in a **(4)** _____ way, but we still have fun.

Your friend,
Tony

Patrick Hall
737 Spring Street
Stamford, CT 06901

Dear Grandpa,

Our ship was in a big storm. It seemed like it would **(5)** _____ the deck into tiny bits. My friend said the ship could be **(6)** _____ by big waves. The storm didn't get that bad! Mom wants calm waters, but that **(7)** _____ happens. Write to me!

Your grandson,
Tony

Grandpa and Grandma
1516 Allen Street
Hudson Falls, NY 12839

MY HOME IS SHIPSHAPE

by Susan Blackaby • illustrated by Doug Bowles

Fifth grade turned out to be the best year of my life! My dad got a job on a ship at the University at Sea. In the program, college students apply from all over the United States to spend a year on a ship. The ship is a lot like a regular campus. It even has a library. What a way to find out what the world is like! You get a firsthand look at other lands. You learn history, which my dad teaches. You get to see amazing art up close. You can study beliefs and customs. Mom and I were so lucky! The families of the professors don't always get to go. ❶

Stop and Think

❶ What can you tell about the narrator?

I can tell that the narrator _____

_____

_____

The professors and their families all bunked on one deck. Mom and Dad had a cozy cabin, and I stayed in a cabin I shared with Kyle. He came from Dallas, and his dad was teaching French. Kim was across the hallway. She came from Denver, and her mom was the math professor. The three of us really hit it off.

There were 450 college students on the trip. They lived on the decks below us. They could get pretty rowdy! We may have gotten a bit wild, too, but most of the time we did our best to act in a dignified way. **2**

Stop and Think

2 What do you learn about the characters?

I learn that the characters _____

_____

_____

At first, we all felt queasy. The ship rocked and rocked, and we didn't have our sea legs yet.

Mom told us she would like the sea to be like a sheet of glass from the ship to the horizon. Kim agreed. But the sea was seldom that still.

"These waves are puny," said Kyle. "Think what will happen if a storm hits. Ships can be broached by giant waves." We teased Kyle because he had a big case of nerves and slept in his life jacket for the first three weeks. **3**

Stop and Think

3 How could the sea be like a sheet of glass?

The sea could _____

_____

_____

I felt seasick at first, but I never felt homesick. My pals back home were riding the bus to school and sitting in class for hours. I was sailing on a ship to see the world!

Kyle, Kim, and I *did* have to study. Parents on the trip conducted classes. At home, I didn't like studying a bunch of dusty facts. On the ship, classes were interesting. We got to read charts and maps and study the stars. When the ship docked, we visited museums, looked at wild plants and animals, and studied history on the exact spot it happened. It was fantastic! **4**

Stop and Think

4 How are classes on a ship different from classes on land? Explain.

On a ship, classes are _____

_____

_____

Every day at sea we kept daily logs. At first we had plenty to say, but when we got used to sailing, one day at sea could be a lot like the next. We ran out of things to report.

"Friday, October ninth," said Kyle. "We're on a ship. What else?"

"All is quiet," Kim said, and turned to me. "What does your log entry say, Tony?"

"'Our home is shipshape,'" I read.

Just then, a blinding flash ripped across the sky. Thunder clapped loudly, and rain pelted the ship so hard that it seemed as if the deck would shatter into tiny bits. **5**

Stop and Think

5 What facts might you include in a daily log?

I might include _____

_____

_____

We scrambled below deck, and Mom met us at the cabins.

"Good idea to come in," she told us. "Why don't you kids just stay below? It's raining like crazy out there!"

Out of the rain, we were fine but our papers got soaked. Kyle set his soggy log by the heater. "When it gets dry, I'll have plenty to say," he told us.

"Set it a little farther over," said Mom. "It's risky to put an inflammable object like that next to the vent."

"Flames would be *big* news," said Kim. **6**

Stop and Think

6 What do you think Kyle will write in his log entry?

I think Kyle will write _____

_____

_____

When the rainstorm had passed, we went up on deck, surprised to see that the sky had cleared and the sun was shining. It was just another lazy day at sea.

"Where were we?" Kyle asked, pulling out his log entry.

"*All was quiet,*" Kim recited. We grinned at how quickly that had reversed.

"Our home was shipshape," I said, "and it still is!" **7**

Stop and Think

7 How is their home still shipshape?

Their home is still shipshape because _____

_____

_____

Think Critically

1. What happens in the story? Copy the chart, and fill it in. PLOT

Characters	Setting
Tony, Kyle, Kim, Mom	University at Sea ship

Plot Events

1. Tony and his pals write in their daily logs.
2.
3.
4.

2. Why does the author tell the story from Tony's point of view?
AUTHOR'S PURPOSE

The author tells the story from Tony's point of view

because _____

_____

_____

_____

3. Why does Tony's attitude toward school change? CAUSE AND EFFECT

Tony's attitude toward school changes because _____

_____

_____

_____

bellowing

betrayed

escapades

outcast

reputation

unfathomable

withered

yearning

Vocabulary

Build Robust Vocabulary

Write the Vocabulary Word that completes each sentence. The first one has been done for you.

One of the best tall tales is about the adventures of a sailor named Salty. The man was so big that he reached the skies. Many sailors like to tell stories of his **(1)** _____escapades_____ . Salty had quite a **(2)** _____ on the high seas. He was known for being bigger than life.

Just how big was Salty? Think of a huge watermelon next to a shrunken and **(3)** _____ grape. If a normal man was the size of the grape, Salty would have been the melon.

Salty was loud, too! Before he learned to speak in low tones, his **(4)** _____ sounds scared everyone he met.

Salty often got looks of fear and spite that

(5) _____ what many were

thinking about him. Some people refused to talk to

him. Salty was an **(6)** _____ .

He wanted to be a sailor, but Salty was so big that no

ship could hold him.

Salty kept on **(7)** _____ to be

at sea. One day, Salty said he *would* sail the seas. This

was **(8)** _____ to the sailors at

the time. How could he fit on any ship?

Then Salty had a huge ship made just for him.

After that, he lived a sailor's life!

Write the Vocabulary Word that best completes the synonym web.

9.

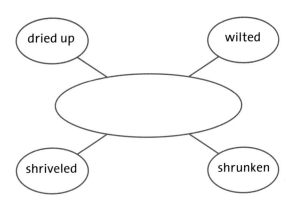

dried up

wilted

shriveled

shrunken

Salty on the High Seas

by Susan Blackaby

illustrated by Jill Newton

Are you yearning for a good story? If you travel near any port in the world, keep your ears open for tall tales. The best ones tell of the escapades of a sailor named Salty. Salty had quite a reputation on the high seas. He was bigger than life. In fact, he was as big as a grizzly bear on the night he was born. As a grown man, Salty was so big that he used a ship's oar to pick his teeth!

As a sailor, Salty was something of an outcast. He was so big that no ship could hold him. ❶

Stop and Think

❶ Why is Salty bigger than life?

Salty is bigger than life because _____

_____

_____

So Salty had a huge ship made just for him. He steered that ship, *Bright Courser*, right around the world. In every port, he made a big splash.

On one trip, the ship sat stalled off the coast of a mighty land mass because the wind refused to blow. At that time, South America and Africa formed one continent.

After three weeks without even a slight breeze, the sailors longed for the sight of the winds filling the sails. Among sailors, this lack of wind was called "the doldrums." **2**

Stop and Think

2 What causes the doldrums?

The doldrums is caused by _____

_____

_____

"We need a big breeze so that we can get going," Salty said. "I'm supposed to be in India right now. Bags of nutmeg and pepper are piled high on the dock. I hate being tied up here night and day."

All of a sudden a light bulb went on in Salty's brain. "All hands on deck!" he cried. Salty's bellowing shout broke glass from Florida to Bombay. "I have a way to fight these doldrums! If there's no wind, we'll make our own." **3**

Stop and Think

3 Why does Salty need to reach India?

Salty needs to reach India because _____

_____

_____

The first mate frowned, and his look of fright betrayed what the rest were thinking. Salty might be hatching one of his wild plans.

"What do you have in mind, sir?" he asked.

"I'll huff and I'll puff and I'll blow this ship right over the land if I have to," Salty cried.

The men were frightened. Then the first mate gave a slight nod. "That might work. But start slow and just give a light sigh. After all, a blast from you could be a disaster." **4**

Stop and Think

4 Why are the men frightened?

The men are frightened because _____

_____

_____

Salty waved his hand as if batting away flies.

"Stop fussing. A fine, soft puff is all it will take. Then we'll need one big breeze to set us right."

"Sir, I think we just need a light puff."

"Nonsense," said Salty. He breathed in and gave out a sigh. The sail fluttered like a bird in flight. Men scrambled to their posts high in the ropes. Salty sniffed. He snorted. And then a very big, bad thing happened.

Salty sneezed. **5**

Stop and Think

5 What do you think will happen next?

I think that _____

_____

_____

The ship ripped across the water, and it didn't stop when it hit the beach. It split the mighty land mass in two! Salty and his men held on tight as jungle and then grassland skidded by. The sea flowed in to fill the rip.

"I've never seen such a sight!" cried the first mate, who was withered like a dried plant from the big breeze.

"Excuse me," said Salty. "It must have been all that pepper from our last trip. But I was right! We might be in port by nightfall." **6**

Stop and Think

6 What happens after Salty sneezes?

After Salty sneezes, _____

_____

_____

A sailor on the dock met *Bright Courser* when it arrived in India. He was shocked to see Salty and his crew.

"Where did you come from?" he asked. "You're early!"

"We took a short cut," said the first mate.

"Yes," said Salty. "We nosed our way in. By the way, we formed a new continent and tripled the size of the Atlantic."

"That's unfathomable!" said the sailor.

"Not for Salty," said the first mate. "Just hold on tight if he sneezes." **7**

Stop and Think

7 Why does the author use the phrase "nosed our way in"?

The author uses this phrase because _____

_____

_____

32

Think Critically

1. What happens in the tall tale? Copy the story map, and fill it in. PLOT

Characters		Setting

Plot Events
1. *Salty's ship is stuck in the doldrums.*
2. *Salty sneezes.*
3.
4.

2. As a sailor, Salty's size causes many problems. How does he react to these problems? CHARACTER

Salty reacts by _____

_____

_____

3. How can you tell that this is a tall tale? AUTHOR'S PURPOSE

I can tell this is a tall tale because _____

_____

_____

accumulate

elastic

elongates

intricate

replenishing

rigid

underlying

vanish

Vocabulary

Build Robust Vocabulary

Write the Vocabulary Word that completes each sentence in the selection. The first one has been done for you.

Without water, life on our planet would not be possible. All life, from simple organisms to the most

(1) _____**intricate**_____ ones, depend on water.

The amazing thing about water is that it exists in three states. When it gets very cold, its molecules slow down. Then it becomes **(2)** _____ and frozen. This is water's solid stage. When energy from the sun warms the frozen water, it melts. This is its liquid form. When it gets hot, the water will turn to steam and

(3) _____ . You may not see water in this gas form, but it's there. It's in the air around you as water vapor.

Water is **(4)** _____ , which means it can stretch out. You can see this as you watch a drop of water sliding down a window pane. It **(5)** _____ , or becomes longer, as it moves.

Water is found everywhere. In its liquid form, it can **(6)** _____ in large puddles after a rain. In its frozen form, it can fall to make layer upon layer of snow. Each **(7)** _____ layer is frozen water.

The water supply on our planet stays the same. It changes forms, but the supply is always **(8)** _____ itself. When the rains come, our creeks and rivers swell, and much of it finds its way back to the sea.

WATER ON OUR PLANET

by Susan Blackaby • illustrated by Gary LaCoste

Water flows under bridges. It rages down rivers and plunges over waterfalls. It crashes in giant waves on the beach. It splashes over a large part of our planet. Out of the tap, it may not seem like a big deal. After all, it's clear. It has no smell. It has no taste. And yet without it, life on our planet would not be possible. In fact, water is what gives our planet the edge. **1**

Water is called H_2O. It's made up of two hydrogen atoms and one oxygen atom. The plus and minus charges attract.

Stop and Think

1 What do you already know about the importance of water?

I already know that _____

_____

_____

Like all things, water is made up of molecules. Most liquids tend to flatten out to make a film. The way the atoms in a water molecule are arranged makes the molecules clump together. They form rounded drops. A drop is a very small amount of water. However, it has a huge number of molecules.

What makes water so amazing? For one thing, water exists in three states. When water freezes, the molecules slow down and get rigid. This is water's solid stage. Energy from the sun heats up the frozen water. It turns into a liquid. When it gets hot, water turns to steam, which is a gas. **2**

Stop and Think

2 What causes water to turn from a solid to a liquid?

Water turns from a solid to a liquid when _____

_____

_____

Water molecules clump together to form drops. The drops are sticky. They stick to glass, cloth, and even this page of paper.

Water is elastic. Think about how a drop drips down a window pane. It begins as a small, round ball. Then it changes shape. As it slides, it elongates. It stretches into the shape of a teardrop. It keeps stretching until it is like a large ribbon. Then the ribbon splits apart. New drops form. These new round drops begin to stretch and slide down the glass. ❸

Water drops slide down windows like ribbons, sometimes splitting apart.

Stop and Think

❸ What happens when water drips down a window? Summarize.

When water drips down a window _____

_____

_____

A lot of the things that water can do seem like strange magic tricks. It can seep into small cracks and creases. It can travel up a wick. It can edge up the sides of a glass. It can travel up the stem of a plant to reach the leaves.

Water can carve out a rock ledge on a cliff. It can act like a giant dredge to create a gorge or canyon. When it rains, water can accumulate to make a gigantic puddle. Then it will vanish when the sun comes out. **4**

Stop and Think

4 What do you think causes the water to vanish?

I think that _____

_____

_____

Where does the water in the puddle go? It evaporates, or changes to vapor. Water molecules float in the air in the form of gas. They stick to things that are cold and condense, or turn back to liquid. For example, drops will form on the outside of a cold drink glass.

In the morning, you can see that water in the air has settled on the grass, trees, and bushes. If it's cold outside, the water will form frost. When the sun shines, the water changes back to vapor. **5**

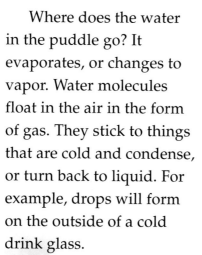

Stop and Think

5 Why does water settle on grass at night?

Water settles on grass at night because _____

_____

_____

The water supply on our planet stays the same. The molecules keep changing, but the supply is always replenishing itself. Most of the water is stored in the sea. It heats up and evaporates. The vapor rises. Then it hits cold air. The molecules stick together. They make clouds. The clouds drift over the land. Some of the water molecules fall to the ground. Raindrops swell creeks. They send rivers raging back to the sea. Intricate snowflakes fall on peaks. The peaks store an underlying layer of frozen water. **6**

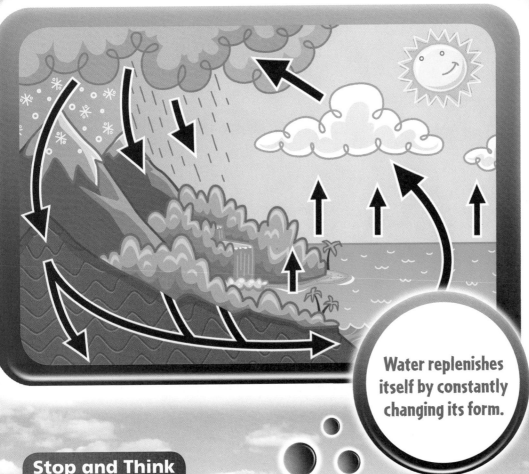

Water replenishes itself by constantly changing its form.

Stop and Think

6 What happens after water vapor hits cold air?

After water vapor hits cold air, _____

_____

_____

Think about water the next time you weed your garden, play soccer on wet grass, or plunge into a cold lake. Water molecules are all around you, and they're on the go. The water in your bean plants may have been in a puddle on a street in Germany! The water soaking into your sneakers may have been frozen in a high ridge. The water drop on the tip of your nose may have lapped at the edge of a warm beach. When it comes to water, stranger things have happened! **7**

Stop and Think

7 How do you think the author feels about water?

I think the author feels that _____

_____

_____

Think Critically

1. What causes water to evaporate? Copy the organizer, and fill it in. **CAUSE AND EFFECT**

Cause		Effect
	→	*Water evaporates.*

2. How does our water supply stay the same? **MAIN IDEA AND DETAILS**

Our water supply stays the same by _____

_____

_____

_____

3. Compare the three stages of water. How are they different?
   COMPARE AND CONTRAST

Here is how they are different: _____

_____

_____

_____

analyzing

basking

damage

detect

sleek

vital

Vocabulary

Build Robust Vocabulary

Write the Vocabulary Word that completes each sentence in the letters. The first one has been done for you.

Dear Crystal,

Yesterday, I went with my mom to a meeting about frogs. The speaker, Dr. Janet Phillips, told us how she has been

(1) _____analyzing_____ data about frogs. She does this

to find out why the frogs are having a hard time surviving.

She said that when we harm the land, we hurt the frogs, too.

When we (2) _____ habitats, we make it hard for

them to survive.

Next weekend, Mom and I will go out to the wetlands at night.

We'll count the frogs we see and hear. Do you want to come with us?

Your pal,

Carlos

Dear Crystal,

My trip with Mom out to the wetlands was amazing! We were able to **(3)** _____ all kinds of frog sounds. We even heard a bullfrog! At one point, I noticed a **(4)** _____ green shape that streaked across the water. It had to be a frog because there are no fish there.

I wish you could have gone with us, Crystal. It was very exciting.

Your pal,
Carlos

Dear Crystal,

I've been thinking about frogs for days. Do you remember, years ago, when we saw a lot of frogs **(5)** _____ in the sun? I want to see that again. That won't happen unless we take steps to protect their habitats.

It's very important for us to take care of the land. I'm going to start telling everyone how **(6)** _____ it is. Would you like to help me ?

Your pal,
Carlos

Can You Hear the Frogs?

by Brad Lewis
illustrated by Pam Johnson

To Carlos, it seemed a little phony, but he went with his mother to the meeting anyway. She said her boss's nephew had attended last week and liked it. At this meeting, they'd be taught how to hear frogs, something that Carlos believed he already knew how to do.

Dr. Janet Phillips started the meeting by saying she had been analyzing data on the number of frogs in towns around Chicago. Dr. Phillips pointed at a bar graph. The graph looked like steps going down. Carlos could see the frogs were having a hard time surviving. **1**

Stop and Think

1 What does the bar graph show?

The bar graph shows _____

_____

_____

Dr. Phillips said amphibians like frogs are delicate. How well they survive can tell us a lot about our habitats. Helpers all over the world were keeping a count of frogs. Meetings like this were the first phase. Everyone would find out about the frogs, and then they could help with the count.

Carlos had heard enough. He wanted to be part of this. He wanted there to be more frogs basking in the sun. He took notes while the room rang with trills and croaks. Dr. Phillips was playing frog calls on a tape recorder. ❷

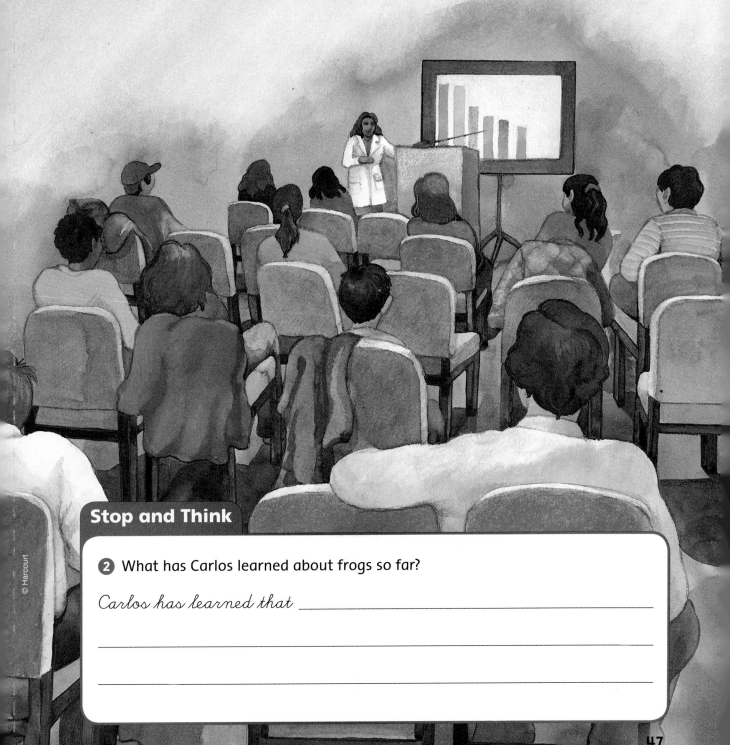

Stop and Think

❷ What has Carlos learned about frogs so far?

Carlos has learned that _____

_____

_____

Carlos left the meeting holding a frog-counting kit that had maps, charts, and photos of different frogs. Dr. Phillips had marked ten wetlands spots for him to visit.

The next evening was just right for frog counting, damp and warm with no wind. Carlos and his mother piled into the car and drove out to find the wetlands on their map. The next phase had begun.

On the trip, they played a tape of frog sounds. Twangs and chirps filled the car. "Frog tunes!" Carlos joked, and they both laughed. **3**

Stop and Think

3 Why do Carlos and his mother play a tape of frog sounds?

They play the tape because _____

_____

_____

© Harcourt

They found seats near the muddy pond Dr. Phillips had marked as a prime spot to detect frog songs. They took care not to damage the land. They had to be very still and quiet.

Later, Carlos saw a sleek streak of green and heard a *Plop!* It must have been a frog, because Dr. Phillips said there were no fish here. Fish eat frog eggs and tadpoles. Soon a phantom foghorn sounded from the middle of the pond. "Bullfrog," Carlos whispered, and he put it down in his log. His mother nodded, chuckling softly. **4**

Stop and Think

4 What do you think might happen if they damage the land?

If they damage the land, then _____

_____

_____

Carlos and his mother visited five spots that night. They were about to leave for home, when Carlos sat back down and put his finger to his lips. He had heard a quacking call. The quacks came faster and faster, from a log nearby. It might be a wood frog, and wood frogs were rare.

His mother pointed to the tape recorder in his pack, so Carlos grabbed it and held up the microphone. The frog's music went on and on. He hoped the microphone was capturing all of it. **5**

Stop and Think

5 How do you think Carlos feels?

I think Carlos feels _____

_____

_____

The following day, Carlos and his mother took their tape to Dr. Phillips. Dr. Phillips played the tape and put some numbers on a graph, then she made a phone call. Carlos and his mother both heard the phrase, "no laughing matter." They exchanged looks. Did they do something wrong?

When Dr. Phillips hung up the phone, she was frowning. She asked Carlos if he was positive the tape recorder's microphone worked. Carlos told her he knew the microphone worked because he had tested it himself. **6**

Stop and Think

6 What do you think will happen next?

I think that _____

_____

_____

"Our graphs tell us that the number of frogs in that pond is going down too fast," Dr. Phillips said. "It's vital that we find out what's going on.

"However, that tape you made is a real trophy. I'm convinced that it's a wood frog." Dr. Phillips smiled. "If so, the town will have more reason to take care of that pond and save all the frogs. You've done a good deed, Carlos."

And to think Carlos expected that meeting to be phony! His feeling of triumph couldn't be more real. **7**

Stop and Think

7 How do you think the author feels about frogs?

I think the author feels _____

_____

_____

Think Critically

1. **What happens in the story? Copy the chart, and fill in the Summary column.** PLOT

Ideas	Summary
• Carlos attends a meeting on frogs. • Carlos and his mom count frogs at a pond. • They record frog sounds and take it to Dr. Phillips. • They learn that the frogs are in danger.	

2. **Now that Carlos has found a rare wood frog, how do you think other frogs will be affected? Explain.** CAUSE AND EFFECT

I think that other frogs will _____

_____

_____

_____

3. **What do you think the author wants you to learn from this story?** AUTHOR'S PURPOSE

I think the author wants me to learn _____

_____

_____

_____

cumbersome

deflated

enraptured

enterprising

monopolize

somberly

stammers

Vocabulary

Build Robust Vocabulary

Write the Vocabulary Word that completes each sentence. The first one has been done for you.

Milena is unhappy each time she has to cross Elm Street.

She looks **(1)** _____ somberly _____ down the street,

waiting for a pause in traffic so she can cross.

When Milena gets to Will's house, she is still nervous

and out of breath. She **(2)** _____ a

little as she complains about the problem on Elm Street.

Will thinks that they are two **(3)** _____

fifth-graders who can get the city to put in a crosswalk.

Milena and Will come up with a plan to get a crosswalk put on Elm Street. This project might **(4)** _____ all their time for a while, but it will be worth it.

The next day, they tell their teacher what they want to do. Their teacher is **(5)** _____ by their plan. "Wow! That's terrific!"

After school, Milena and Will are on the sidewalk beside Elm Street. They each have a **(6)** _____ backpack full of books on their back. They have homework to do, but they stop off to try and get some support from other residents. They find that no one wants to help them with their plan. They feel **(7)** _____ .

Write the Vocabulary Word that best completes the synonym web.

8.

delighted

entranced

enchanted

thrilled

Elm Street Speaks!

by Margie Sigman • illustrated by John Haslam

CHARACTERS

Milena, *a fifth-grade girl*   **Mr. Steadman,** *a teacher*

Will, *a fifth-grade boy*   **Amy Wong,** *a resident*

Officer Simms, *an officer of the law*

Stop and Think

1 How do you know that this is a play?

I know that this is a play because _____

_____

_____

ACT 1

SETTING: *Inside a residence on Elm Street.*

TIME: *The present.*

MILENA: (*Walks through the door, shaking a sodden umbrella.*) The weather is lousy out there! It took me forever to cross Elm Street, as usual. It's like crossing the runway of a big-city airport! We need a crosswalk, *now!*

WILL: We've been saying that for months. Let's do something meaningful, instead of just complaining.

MILENA: Like what?

WILL: The kids on Threadtree Lane demanded their own park. They wrote letters to the newspaper editor and the city council. It took a lot of effort, but now they have a terrific community park.

MILENA: Well, I'm ready to try anything. ❷

Stop and Think

❷ What is the problem on Elm Street?

The problem is that _____

_____

_____

ACT 2

TIME: *Three days later.*

SETTING: *A fifth-grade classroom.*

MR. STEADMAN: Are you two making steady progress with your Elm Street project?

MILENA: *(Looking deflated.)* I can't convince one person in this community to produce a letter demanding a crosswalk.

WILL: I bet Milena and I talked to a hundred Elm Street residents!

MR. STEADMAN: Did you compose a letter yet?

MILENA: I already started mine. *(Begins reading from a paper.)* "My name is Milena Garza and I'm in fifth grade. Every day I face extreme danger from heavy traffic on my own street!" ❸

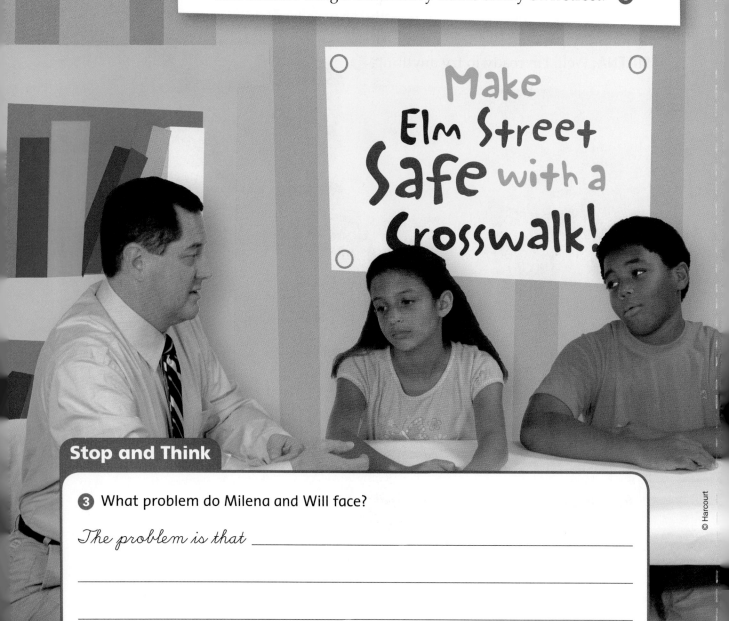

Stop and Think

❸ What problem do Milena and Will face?

The problem is that _____

_____

_____

MR. STEADMAN: That's a fantastic beginning, Milena.

WILL: *(Slaps his forehead.)* I almost forgot! I had a major brainstorm last night while I was watching TV. What Milena read is fine, but there's a better way for us to spread the message about Elm Street!

MILENA: *(Looking puzzled.)* What do you mean?

WILL: In here's our secret weapon! *(Picks up a heavy, cumbersome backpack and reveals a video camera.)*

MR. STEADMAN: A video! What a great idea! ❹

Stop and Think

❹ How do you think the video camera will be used?

I think that _____

_____

_____

ACT 3

TIME: *The next afternoon.*

SETTING: *On a sidewalk on Elm Street. MILENA is standing next to AMY WONG. WILL is holding the camera steady.*

MILENA: Amy, I just saw you running across Elm Street. I don't want to monopolize your time, but we are trying to get a crosswalk installed on this street. What do you think?

AMY: *(Clutches her chest as she catches her breath.)* I think that's a fantastic idea. Should crossing the street be a life or death trip? This traffic is frightening!

MILENA: Thank you very much for your time, Amy. *(Speaks somberly in a deep voice.)* Amy Wong won't feel safe until the authorities install a crosswalk here. Okay, cut, Will! ❺

Stop and Think

❺ Why is Amy so out of breath?

Amy is so out of breath because _____

_____

_____

ACT 4

TIME: *The next day.*

SETTING: *Back in the classroom.*

WILL: *(Sounding excited.)* Yesterday after breakfast we started to film. The weather was sunny and pleasant, so we were lucky.

MILENA: Will already got several awesome shots of the heavy traffic on Elm Street. There was a steady line of people wanting to talk to us, too.

OFFICER SIMMS: *(Surprising the students.)* May I interrupt? Hi, I'm Officer Simms. Mr. Steadman told me about your video. You kids have been working hard! I bet you're the most enterprising fifth graders in Featherton. We've had three accidents on Elm Street this year, so I'm more than ready to support your efforts. **6**

Make
Elm Street
Safe with a
Crosswalk!

Stop and Think

6 What happened yesterday to make Will excited?

Yesterday, _____

_____

_____

WILL: *(Stammers a little with excitement.)* We have kids, moms, and dads telling their own stories on film.

OFFICER SIMMS: When you finish up your video, let's head to city hall. No one will believe what you've done. We're going to spread the word and get some things changed in this community, thanks to you.

MILENA: *(Enraptured.)* Wow! Elm Street speaks!

(Lights fade and a spotlight comes up on the Elm Street banner.) **7**

Make
Elm Street
Safe with a
Crosswalk!

Stop and Think

7 How do you think the author feels about the role of kids in a community?

I think the author feels that _____

_____

_____

© Harcourt

Think Critically

1. What happened in the play? Copy the chart, and fill in the Summary column. **PLOT**

Ideas	Summary
• Milena and Will want a crosswalk on Elm Street. • They can't convince people to write letters. • They interview people crossing Elm Street. • Officer Simms agrees to help them.	

2. How did using the video camera affect events in the story? **CAUSE AND EFFECT**

Using the video camera caused _____

_____

_____

3. What would you like to change in your community? How can you help make this change happen? **PERSONAL RESPONSE**

I would like _____

_____

To help make this happen, I can _____

_____

_____

acclimate

accustomed

essential

secure

streamlined

summit

Vocabulary

Build Robust Vocabulary

Write the Vocabulary Word that completes each sentence. The first one has been done for you.

Earth is surrounded by a blanket of air called the *atmosphere*. The lowest layer, about 7.5 miles thick, is higher than the **(1)** _____ summit _____ of the tallest mountain. This layer contains 90 percent of our planet's air. All of our weather changes take place here.

Without help, no one can live beyond this lower layer of atmosphere. But some men and women do go beyond it—into space. They are taken there by rockets with **(2)** _____ designs. A great deal of force is needed to lift heavy rockets beyond the atmosphere and into space.

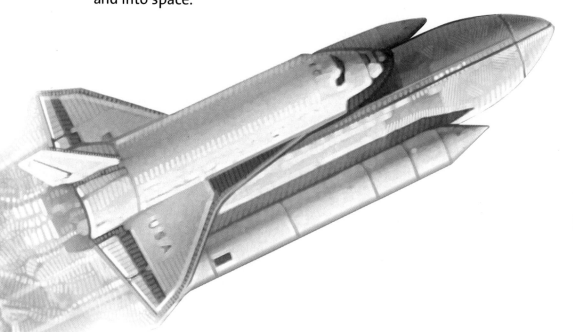

Astronauts go to the International Space Station (ISS) 220 miles above Earth. They must quickly get **(3)** _____ to life there. Astronauts study many things in space. One thing they want to know is how plants, animals, and humans **(4)** _____ to life without gravity.

To keep muscles strong, it is **(5)** _____ to exercise while in space. Sleeping bags must be hooked to a wall to stay **(6)** _____ . Imagine trying to sleep if your bag kept drifting through the cabin, bumping into things!

Write the Vocabulary Word that best completes the synonym web.

7.

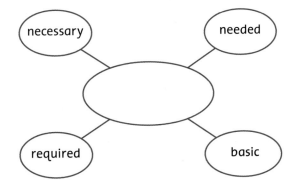

necessary

needed

required

basic

Life in Space

by Jeff Putnam • illustrated by Eric Williams

Have you ever thought about making your home in space? Some people do live in space. Someday, you could, too.

Home, Sweet Home

Our home is a huge globe surrounded by endless space. We call it Earth. A blanket of air called the *atmosphere* surrounds Earth. The atmosphere allows us to breathe and protects us from the extreme heat of the sun. During the night, it protects us from the terrible cold of space. The lowest layer, higher than the summit of the tallest mountain in the world, is about 7.5 miles (12 kilometers) thick. This layer contains 90 percent of Earth's air, as well as its weather. It's impossible to live beyond this lowest layer—without help. **1**

Stop and Think

1 What do you want to know about life in space?

I want to know _____

_____

_____

Getting into Space

The first hurdle to jump is just getting into space! Powerful, streamlined rockets carry people into space. They burn fuel and produce hot gases, which boost them into space.

Sometimes, the rocket carries a smaller craft called a shuttle. Shuttles make more than one trip; rockets don't. The shuttle separates from the rocket, and the rocket's parts fall back to Earth. Then the shuttle, with trained astronauts aboard, continues its trip into space.

Next stop—the International Space Station (ISS), a laboratory in space! **2**

Stop and Think

2 What do you think you will learn about next?

I think I will learn about _____

_____

_____

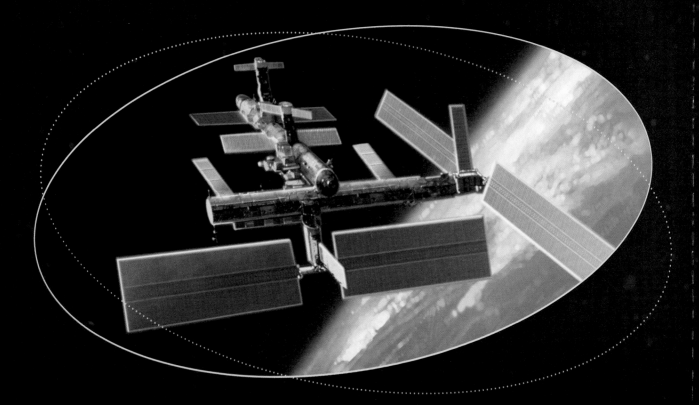

Wait For Me!

The ISS is really moving! To catch it, be ready to match its speed of 17,000 miles (27,350 kilometers) per hour. It's way up there, too—220 miles (352 kilometers) above Earth. But you finally reach it and dock. Climb through the hatches, and you're ready to settle down in space.

Your New Home

Your new home in space is enormous. The ISS is almost as long as a football field and weighs about a million pounds (453,600 kilograms). Engineers from around the world put it together over several years. The different pieces were constructed on Earth, then flown up and pieced together in space. **3**

Stop and Think

3 How does the author make you feel about traveling in space?

The author makes me feel _____

_____

_____

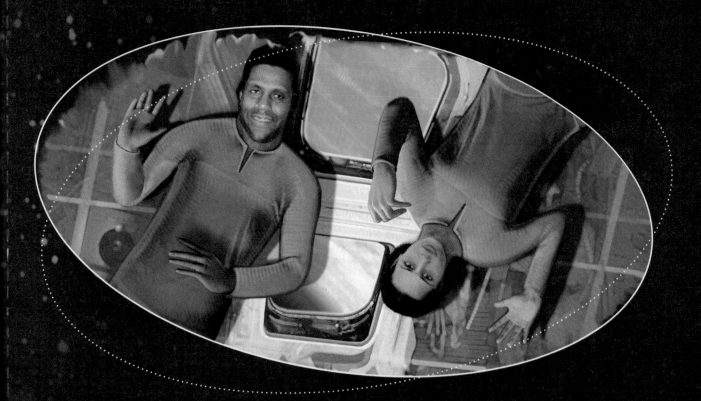

How Is Space Different from Earth?

For one thing, you're weightless in space. There's no gravity, so you float around the cabin. The problem is, so does everything else! You have to avoid bumping into other astronauts and strap down both your food and nonfood items. Drinking without a straw is very impractical in space. And don't even try taking a shower—it's impossible!

Daily Life in Space

Astronauts living in space do lots of tests. Before take-off, they prepare experiments. Once in space, they study plants to see how they grow. They raise mice, chicks, spiders, frogs, and other nonhuman passengers to see how they acclimate to life without gravity. ④

Stop and Think

④ Which words on this page contain prefixes meaning "not," "no," or "the opposite of"? Underline them.

Words that contain these prefixes are _____

_____

Living in space requires lots of equipment. Here's a preview of some of the things you might need.

Sleeping bag – It hooks to a wall so you're secure and immobile.

Space toys – During nonwork times, astronauts play with balls, jacks, marbles, and even a yo-yo.

Space music – Jamming in space is cool! But it's impolite to play when anyone is trying to sleep.

Slippers – Maybe you already have a pair just like these. Bring them along! **5**

Stop and Think

5 Why do you think living in space requires lots of equipment?

I think it requires lots of equipment because _____

_____

_____

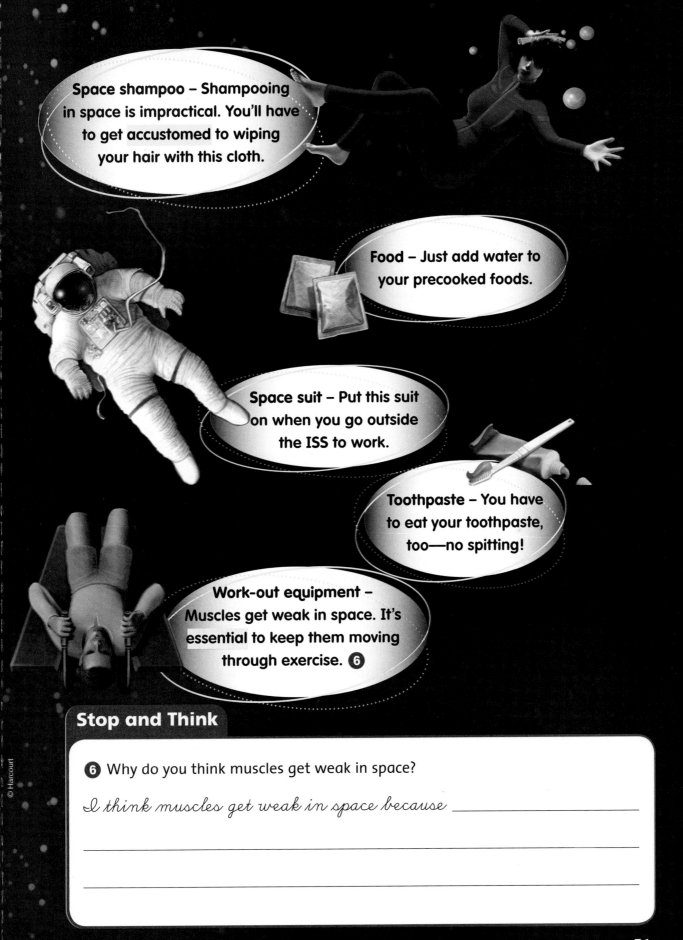

Space shampoo – Shampooing in space is impractical. You'll have to get **accustomed** to wiping your hair with this cloth.

Food – Just add water to your precooked foods.

Space suit – Put this suit on when you go outside the ISS to work.

Toothpaste – You have to eat your toothpaste, too—no spitting!

Work-out equipment – Muscles get weak in space. It's **essential** to keep them moving through exercise. **6**

Stop and Think

6 Why do you think muscles get weak in space?

I think muscles get weak in space because _____

_____

_____

The Future in Space

What is the future of life in space? Can you picture a hotel in space? Don't dismiss it as nonsense. How about a space wedding? Can you picture a mine on the moon or on Mars? Maybe a fish farm? These ideas aren't impossible. They may seem improbable, but each could happen in the future. Today's space researchers are working nonstop to come up with new ideas for life in space. Maybe you'll be the one to test out their ideas. Oh, and don't forget your slippers! **7**

Stop and Think

7 Are the author's statements about future life in space facts or opinions? Explain your answer.

The statements about future life in space are _____

_____

_____

Think Critically

1. What have you learned about life in space? Copy the chart, and fill in the third column. **MAIN IDEA AND DETAILS**

K	W	L

2. How is life in the space station different from life on Earth? **COMPARE AND CONTRAST**

Here is how life in the space station is different:

_____

_____

_____

3. Do you think you would like to live in space? Explain. **PERSONAL RESPONSE**

I think that _____

_____

_____

cramped

ignited

jettisoned

potentially

squinting

tranquility

Vocabulary

Build Robust Vocabulary

Write the Vocabulary Word that completes each sentence in the selection. The first one has been done for you.

In 1768, Captain James Cook led a mission from England to Tahiti. His job was to see how long it took the planet Venus to pass in front of the Sun. This information would (1) _____potentially_____ help researchers figure out the distance from the Sun to Earth.

With ninety-five crew members and all their supplies, Cook's ship was very (2) _____ when it set out from England. Because the ship was made of wood, crew members had to be very careful with fire. The ship could be (3) _____ if any crew member was careless.

Cook and his crew were glad to get to Tahiti. The

(4) _____ of the island was a peaceful relief

after months at sea.

Cook began observing Venus on June 3, 1769. He was

(5) _____ into a telescope, trying to time

Venus's trip across the Sun. But the outline of Venus was too

fuzzy. It was hard to tell exactly when the planet's trip across the

Sun began and ended. There was a great deal of confusion. In the

end, the whole project had to be scrapped.

Cook continued exploring the South Pacific. He wanted to

make accurate maps of the area. At one point, he collided with the

Great Barrier Reef. The ship took on water, and all heavy objects had

to be **(6)** _____ so the ship wouldn't sink. You

will read more about Cook's adventures in "To the South Pacific."

TO THE SOUTH PACIFIC

by Linda Barr • illustrated by Cathy Morrison

Every 120 years, the planet Venus passes in front of the Sun. This event is called the Transit of Venus. It can be seen from only a few places on Earth.

In 1768, researchers in England were preparing for the Transit of Venus in 1769. They wanted to send out people to observe the Transit from different places. One of these places was Tahiti in the South Pacific. But they were unclear about its exact location.

The researchers hoped to use the Transit of Venus to figure out the distance from the Sun to Earth. They planned to find out how far the remaining planets were from the Sun. **1**

Stop and Think

1 Why is observing the Transit of Venus important?

It's important because _____

_____

_____

The South Pacific was a tricky place to navigate. In 1768, there were few maps of the South Seas. Some mapmakers thought there was a giant continent in this area. Others didn't agree.

Tahiti is only twenty miles wide, a tiny speck in the vast seas. To reach it, a ship would have to cross thousands of miles of open water. Potentially, the ship could miss Tahiti completely.

The researchers asked James Cook, an experienced ship captain, to lead the dangerous mission. Cook's ship would sail alone and have no communication with England. It would have no protection from storms. If a fire ignited on board, the wooden ship would go up in flames. ❷

ENGLAND

TAHITI

James Cook's Voyage

Stop and Think

❷ Is the mission really dangerous? Explain.

The mission _____

_____

_____

On August 12, 1768, Cook's ship set sail with ninety-five crew members aboard. The cramped ship was filled with as many supplies as it could hold. The crew wouldn't be able to get any more food or water during the long trip across the seas.

From England, the ship sailed in a westerly direction and crossed the Atlantic. As it rounded the tip of South America, five men died in a storm. The ship sailed for ten more weeks across the South Pacific. The crew's food supply slowly disappeared. They had to catch fish to avoid starvation. ❸

Stop and Think

❸ What do you want to know about Cook's mission?

I want to know _____

_____

_____

After eight long months, the ship finally reached Tahiti. The location was truly beautiful, causing much celebration among the crew. Tahiti was a vision of peace and tranquility. It almost took Cook's attention away from the reason for his trip—to witness the Transit of Venus!

Cook's instructions were to time how long this event took. On June 3, 1769, Cook finally made his observations of the Transit. Squinting into a telescope, he watched the motion of a small black disk as it slid across the Sun. But the outline of Venus was too fuzzy. It was hard to tell exactly when the planet's trip across the Sun began and ended. **4**

During the Transit, Venus looks like a tiny black dot sliding across the Sun.

Stop and Think

4 What do you think will happen next?

I think that _____

_____

_____

Around the globe, other observers were also timing the Transit. Many of them recorded different times. This led to a great deal of confusion. It would be 120 more years before anyone could figure out the distances between the planets!

After Tahiti, Cook continued his explorations of the South Pacific, trying to find the legendary Great Southern Continent. It was thought to stretch across most of the southern Pacific and include what is now Australia. In time, Cook confirmed that the smaller continent of Australia was the only one in the South Pacific. Maps showing a giant continent in the South Pacific were now useless. ❺

Here, Cook observed the Transit of Venus.

Stop and Think

❺ How did Cook's explorations affect mapmakers?

Cook's explorations caused _____

_____

_____

During one trip, Cook's ship had a collision with the Great Barrier Reef near what is now Australia. With the ship taking on water, all heavy objects were jettisoned overboard in order to lighten the load. Still, destruction to the ship forced Cook to land on the closest beach. Repairs took ten long weeks.

As Cook sailed, he drew maps of Earth's seas and coasts. With this new information, he made corrections on old maps. **6**

Stop and Think

6 Why does the author describe Cook's collision with the reef?

The author describes this because _____

_____

_____

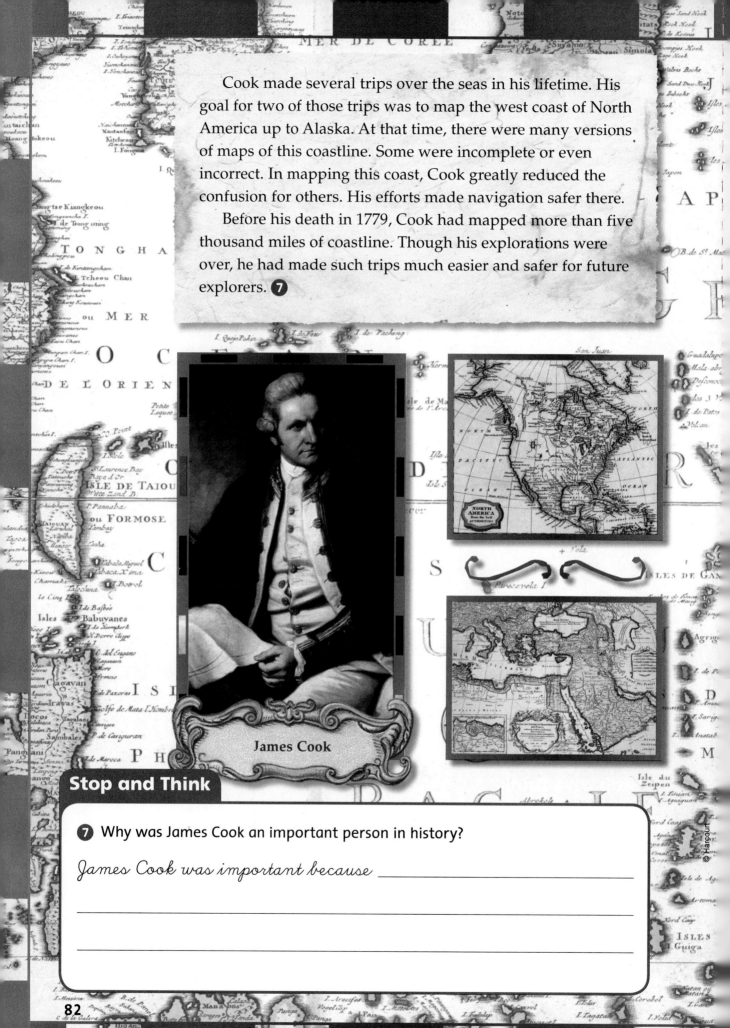

Cook made several trips over the seas in his lifetime. His goal for two of those trips was to map the west coast of North America up to Alaska. At that time, there were many versions of maps of this coastline. Some were incomplete or even incorrect. In mapping this coast, Cook greatly reduced the confusion for others. His efforts made navigation safer there.

Before his death in 1779, Cook had mapped more than five thousand miles of coastline. Though his explorations were over, he had made such trips much easier and safer for future explorers. **7**

James Cook

Stop and Think

7 Why was James Cook an important person in history?

James Cook was important because _____

_____

_____

Think Critically

1. What have you learned about James Cook's explorations? Copy the chart, and fill in the third column. **MAIN IDEA AND DETAILS**

K	W	L

2. How would you describe James Cook? **CHARACTER**

James Cook _____

_____

_____

3. Why are trips to the South Pacific easier and safer today?
CAUSE AND EFFECT

The trips are easier and safer because _____

_____

_____